At the Seaside

By Diane Church

Photographs by Chris Fairclough

W
FRANKLIN WATTS
LONDON•SYDNEY

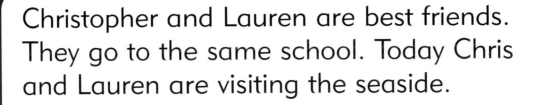

Christopher and Lauren are best friends.
They go to the same school. Today Chris
and Lauren are visiting the seaside.

Chris was born with Down's Syndrome.
This means he finds it harder to
learn things than other children.
This is called a learning difficulty.

While he waits for Lauren to arrive, Chris plays on the computer. He's very excited about going to the seaside. "Can you find the word 'seaside'?" asks his mum. Chris points at the screen. "Well done!" she says.

Chris is learning to read and write and he is doing well at school. He does need extra help so he has a special person who works with him.

Then Chris helps his dad in the garden. "Hurry up, Lauren!" he thinks to himself.

> People with learning difficulties can find it difficult to speak. Chris doesn't speak very clearly but his friends and family understand him.

At last, Lauren arrives. The two friends are soon playing together. "I can't wait to get to the beach," Lauren tells Chris.

"I want to play in the sea," Lauren says. "Me too!" Chris agrees. "Why don't we take your ball with us?" asks Lauren.

Because Chris has Down's Syndrome, his eyes slant a little. Having Down's Syndrome means he might not grow as tall as other children.

Lauren and Chris help to pack the car for the day. "Have we got all we need?" asks Lauren's mum. When everything is ready, they drive to the seaside.

When they arrive, they walk down to the beach. On the way Chris looks through a telescope. "How many seagulls can you see?" asks Lauren. "Five!" Chris shouts.

Although it took him a long time to learn, Chris enjoys counting.

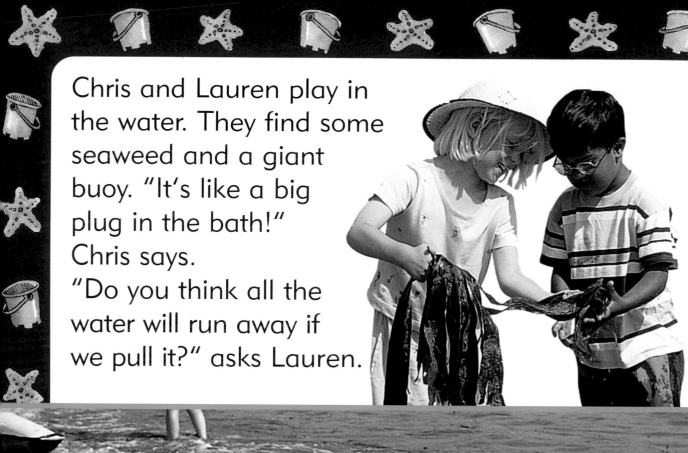

Chris and Lauren play in the water. They find some seaweed and a giant buoy. "It's like a big plug in the bath!" Chris says.
"Do you think all the water will run away if we pull it?" asks Lauren.

Then Chris's mum calls them. "You'll have to get changed if you want to play in the sea," she says. First Chris takes off his t-shirt and his glasses. "We'll take off your hearing aid, too," says his mum.

Some people with Down's Syndrome can have difficulties seeing and hearing, though everyone is different. Chris sometimes wears a hearing aid and glasses to help him.

Chris's mum puts some sun-cream on him to stop the sun burning him. "I need sun-cream, too," Lauren tells her mum.

The two friends play in the water. "It's freezing!" Chris squeals.

They use their
buckets to
carry water up
the beach.

At lunch time the children eat sandwiches from their picnic. "This is great fun!" Chris says.

"I wish we could come to the seaside every day!" adds Lauren.

After lunch they build a
sandcastle. Chris knocks
the sandcastle down.
"Why do you keep knocking
it down?" asks Lauren.
Chris is confused.
"I'm sorry," he says.

Chris gets excited and
sometimes doesn't
understand what
people want him to
do, so he does the
wrong things.

Later Chris and Lauren go to a rock pool with their nets to catch crabs. "I've got one!" calls Lauren. "Oh no!" sighs Chris who keeps dropping them. "You need to scoop them up," Lauren explains.

Like everyone who finds something difficult, Chris can get frustrated and cross.

They put the crab into a bucket.
"What shall we call the crab?"
asks Chris's mum.
"Jaws!" chuckles Chris.
"Now I'll put him back," says his mum.

Next Chris writes his name in the sand. "That's so the seagulls know who I am!" he thinks to himself.

Chris finds it hard to concentrate. He is proud of having learnt to write his name.

As a special treat Chris and Lauren go to the amusement park. On the trampoline it is really hard to stand up. In the end the children have most fun bouncing on their bottoms!

Then they have
an ice-cream.
"This has been
a brilliant
day!" Chris
tells Lauren.

Chris enjoys the same
things as Lauren,
but sometimes it
takes him longer to
learn simple tasks.

On the way home, Lauren and Chris share what they have enjoyed most about their day. "Being with you!" Chris laughs. "You're my best friend!" "And you're my best friend too!" Lauren smiles.

Facts about people with learning difficulties

⭐ People with learning difficulties can do many of the same things as other people – they just take longer to learn them.

⭐ Down's Syndrome is one form of learning difficulty. There are many others. Often, no-one knows why a baby is born with learning difficulties.

⭐ Remember everyone with learning difficulties is different. One person may be able to read and write but another may not. Some will get jobs and live on their own, others will need to be looked after.

⭐ You cannot see learning difficulties. You may only discover that a person has a learning difficulty when you have known them for a long time.

Glossary

Down's Syndrome   a condition that people are born with. It means you look different and find it difficult to learn.

hearing loss   when you can't hear properly and need to wear a hearing aid.

learning difficulties   when someone finds it harder to learn things. It doesn't mean they cannot learn at all, just that it takes longer.

physical disabilities   when someone cannot use parts of their bodies as expected.

sight loss   when you need to wear glasses to help you see properly.

Try to be helpful

1. People with learning difficulties want to be treated the same as everyone else. Make sure you treat them the same as your other friends.

2. Be patient. A person with learning difficulties may take longer to understand what you say to them and how to answer. With a little time, you should be able to understand each other.

3. Listen carefully. A person with learning difficulties may not speak clearly.

4. Some people with learning difficulties need help, others don't. Always remember to ask if a person needs help.

5. Talk to the person and use their name. Just because they have learning difficulties doesn't mean they can't speak for themselves.

6. People with learning difficulties may have the same interests and hobbies as you. You could do them together!

Further information and addresses

Down's Syndrome Association
155 Mitcham Road
London
SW17 9PG
www.downs-syndrome.org.uk

Mencap National Centre
123 Golden Lane
London
EC1Y 0RT

REACH National Advice Centre
for Children with Reading Difficulties
California Country Park
Nine Mile Ride,
Finchampstead, RG40 4HT
www.reach-reading.demon.co.uk

National Council on Intellectual Disability
PO Box 181
Fyshwick
Tennant Street
Auckland 2609
Australia
ncid@peg.apc.aug

Index

© 2000 Franklin Watts

Franklin Watts
96 Leonard Street
London
EC2A 4XD

Franklin Watts Australia
14 Mars Road
Lane Cove
NSW 2066

ISBN: 0 7496 3695 5

Dewey Decimal Classification
Number: 362.4

10 9 8 7 6 5 4 3

A CIP catalogue record for
this book is available from the
British Library.

Printed in Malaysia

Consultants: The Down's Syndrome
Association; Beverley Mathias, REACH.
Editor: Samantha Armstrong
Designer: Louise Snowdon
Photographer: Chris Fairclough
Illustrator: Eliz Hüseyin

With thanks to: Christopher Moorghen
and his family, Lauren Hare and the
Down's Syndrome Association.